101 Ways to Add to Your INCOME

. . .for Young People
. . .for Retirees
. . .for Families
. . .for Everyone.

Dr. Duane R. Lund

Distributed by
Adventure Publications, Inc.
P.O. Box 269
Cambridge, MN 56479

ISBN 0-934860-10-6

Dedication
To my uncle, Verner Anderson, who gave me my first real job and taught me so much about being a good boss.

TABLE OF CONTENTS

Direct Sales - Selling Established Lines of Products
Farrier Service
Garage Sales and Flea Markets
Food Related
Gunsmithing
Home Laundry
Home Barber/Beauty Shop
House Cleaning
Income Tax Service
Interior Decorating
  Consulting
  Decorating
Janitorial Services
Knitting
Leather Work - Shoes/Harnesses
Manufacturing - Small Operations
Modeling and Television Commercials
Office Equipment and Services
Photography
Photo Developing
Picture Framing
Plaques - Trophies - Awards - Engraving
Pollution and Hazardous Waste Testing
Rentals
  Advertising Balloons, Lights and Signs
  Bicycles and Scooters
  Costumes
  Portable Toilets
  Water Associated Rentals
Repair Services
Restoration
  Automobiles
  Boats
  Clocks and Watches
  Houses
  Sandblasting, pressurized water treatment and steam
    cleaning
Security Related
  Locksmith
  Alarm systems
  Vehicle security
  House watching
Sign Making
Specialty Sewing
Swimming Pool and Hot Tub Cleaning and Repair
Taxidermy
Telemarketing
Tile/Carpet Installation
Tool Sharpening
Tree and Shrubbery Care and Removal

Vending Machines
Welding
Window Washing
Wood Products
Yard and Beach Care

PART V *CHILD CARE* / 43

Babysitting
Children of Working Parents (Day Care)
Foster Children
Handicapped Care
Nanny

PART VI *CONSULTANT* / 45

PART VII *ENTERTAINMENT* / 46

Comedian
Disc Jockey
Musical Entertainment
Performing for Parties

PART VIII *GOVERNMENT RELATED* / 48

Assessor
Appraising
Census Taker
City and County Governments
Fireman
Fire Warden
Jury Duty
Officeholder, Elected
Political Party Activity
Poll Taking
Public Libraries
Schools

PART IX *HEALTH RELATED* / 52

Aerobics - Exercise - Fitness
Health Foods
Health Aide
Massage Service
Tanning

PART X *HOME AND PROPERTY INCOME* / 54

Bed and Breakfast
Home Restaurant
Rental
Farm Rentals
Storage

PART XI *NATURE'S BOUNTY* / 56

Christmas Wreaths and Candelabras

PREFACE

A single income is no longer sufficient to sustain most families or even many individuals. In order to enjoy the life style one would prefer, second incomes - usually part time work of some kind - are often necessary.

This book suggests 101 (actually more like 150) ways to add to your income. Many can be family endeavors. In most cases the training and knowledge necessary is easily attained - or you may already have both. The investment is also minimal in most cases.

Because of the large number of suggestions, you may feel a need for further information. We have tried to say where this can be found.

We would suggest that whatever endeavor you choose, make it something you really enjoy, because these will likely be hours spent above and beyond a regular job.

It is advisable to check with your insurance agent to be sure possible liability incurred will be covered.

Good luck! Let us hear your success stories.

PART I
AGRICULTURE RELATED

If you have a green thumb and a love for gardening, agriculture related enterprises may be for you. Most of the possibilities listed in this chapter are designed for gardens, small greenhouses or a limited acreage of land. There is one section (the first), however, which deals with added income for farmers with large acreages.

Most suggestions are focused on a few weeks or months of effort each year. Little capital is required. Your major investment will be time and labor - hopefully a labor of love.

ADDED INCOME FOR FARMERS

There are several possibilities:

1. Many city folks would like the experience of living on a farm - especially for their children or grandchildren. A week or two on an operating farm can be a rewarding vacation. These people want to experience living in a farmhouse, eating their meals with a farm family, and trying hands-on agriculture. Farms with livestock are the most popular. The charge may be comparable to what it would cost to stay at a resort.
2. If your farm includes a fishing lake, many people will pay for the opportunity to fish it. You may charge by the hour or by the pound or some combination thereof.
3. If you can provide duck, goose, pheasant or deer hunting, there are many hunters who will gladly pay for privacy and exclusive hunting privileges.
4. Campground development may also bring you added income. Some campers prefer these smaller, more private campsites. However, some may expect electricity, water, and even sewer hookups. These can be expensive. Also, check with local authorities (county or township) for possible licensing requirements and other regulations.

BEEKEEPING

Here is an interesting hobby with financial rewards. It is not all that difficult to start a colony or to maintain a profitable enterprise, but don't get involved until you have visited a beekeeper and carefully observed the operation. Most university extension services have literature available on the subject and supply houses are willing to help.

Equipment is not expensive, but you will need to purchase such items as:

the initial hives (start with one or two)

supers (placed on top of the brood nest)

frames

queen excluders

smoker

hive tool (to pry the supers apart)

feeders

gloves

bee veil

honey extractor

Beginners outfits are available from supply houses and will include all you need to get started, including the queen and worker bees.

There are a number of diseases and natural enemies to deal with - all the way from wax worms to toads to bears!

Most states require that hives be registered with the state entomologist.

Marketing is an important consideration. As a beginner —

let your friends know you are in the business,

sell from your home,

advertise (at least a yard sign), and

market your own brand through local stores.

As you can see by now, there is far more you need to know about beekeeping than can be contained in this kind of book. If you are interested, your next step is to read the literature and then visit a beekeeping operation.

And if you are allergic to bee stings — forget it!

FISH PONDS — FOR FOOD AND FOR SPORT

Natural ponds or even those created by heavy equipment can produce a profitable crop of fish. Good fishing in lakes and streams is hard to come by these days. People are willing to pay a good price to fish ponds well-stocked with trout, bass, panfish, catfish and even bullheads. Parents are particularly anxious to provide this opportunity for their children — or grandchildren. The charge is usually by the hour with an additional charge for those fish kept.

There is also a good commercial market for fish — particularly trout, perch and catfish. These can be netted or seined from the ponds.

Large ponds or small lakes may generate their own food for the fish, but commercial food is available. Fish add more weight per pound of food consumed than any variety of livestock. Some kinds of fish, like northern pike or walleye, prefer live food — such as minnows. They are, however, slow growing compared to other varieties and relatively difficult to raise.

In cold climates, shallow ponds will freeze out in winter unless aerated. Commercial aerators are available but are fairly expensive; however, old vacuum cleaners with a reversed action will do just fine.

University extension services are usually good sources for further information about growing fish. You should also check with your local Department of Natural Resources regarding possible licensing and other regulations.

FLOWERS

There are several lucrative possibilities:

1. Spring proms and June weddings create a huge short-term market for corsages. A mini-greenhouse specializing in orchids or other corsage flowers can be a good investment. You can sell to floral shops and/or with a little advertising, create a clientele of your own.

2. Grow varieties of flowers in your garden that are usually used in bouquets. Choose a location where they are highly visible to passing traffic. Post a sign inviting customers to stop by. Advise floral shops of what you have available so that they can call on you when they are in short supply. A small greenhouse is also a possibility for year-around marketing. You may want to specialize in a single variety — such as orchids or roses.

3. In the spring of the year, with the help of a small, inexpensive, plastic-covered temporary greenhouse, you can provide homeowners with bedding, flower baskets, etc. You could also include starter vegetable plants, such as tomatoes or peppers. Location and/or advertising are essential to developing a business. You will be in direct competition with greenhouses and nurseries but you will have the great advantage of a much smaller investment, and since you will probably not be hiring outside labor, you should be able to under-sell them and still make a good profit.The season will be short, but that has its advantages in that you will not be tied down for long.

4. Dried flowers have a market. Floral shops may be your best potential customer since they rarely want to bother with the process themselves.

GARDEN CROPS

Fresh garden crops sell at a premium. Just a few acres of well-attended land will yield a good return.

Marketing is the key. It is possible to attract regular customers who will come to you. Roadside stands are another possibility. Smaller grocery stores should also be contacted (large supermarkets often have a year-around purchase agreement with suppliers from southern climates).

Crops may be grown year-around in northern regions in greenhouses, but the cost of heating can be significant. However, even in cold climates, people do make good incomes growing even single crops — such as rhubarb or tomatoes — in greenhouses. Year-around aquaculture* is also worth checking out with your university extension service.

HERBS, SPICES AND BEAN SPROUTS

There are an increasing number of cooks and restaurant chefs who prefer fresh — or even dried — herbs to those sold in a box. They just aren't available in many communities. A typical, backyard garden will grow enough herbs, spices and beansprouts to earn you significant cash. Many of the surplus herbs may be dried and sold at other times of the year.

Begin by experimenting with small patches. You may want to check with your county agent or nearest university extension service for information about which will grow in your area, suggested fertilizer, type of soil, etc.

Here are a few possibilities:

dill	thyme
chives	basil
peppers	rosemary
mint	beansprouts
garlic	sage

Once you are confident you can grow a good product, take samples to local stores and restaurants. Before investing more time and labor, be sure you have a market. However, if stores and restaurants are not interested, flea markets are a possibility. A small ad in the local paper may also bring customers to your door.

Beansprouts for salads and oriental dishes may be grown rather quickly and if you have a market, consider growing them inside during the cold season.

Herbs may be dried in your kitchen oven or by hanging in a dry place. Commercial dryers are available if you have the quantity to justify the investment.

MAPLE SYRUP

Native Americans were manufacturing maple syrup (and sugar) when European explorers first came to North America.

Harvesting techniques were simple but effective. A deep slice was made in the bark of the tree with a knife or tomahawk and a cedar splinter was driven into the wound to serve as a spout. The sap dripped into a birchbark container at the foot of the tree. Before the coming of the trader with his iron kettles, the Indian boiled the sap in clay vessels or by dropping very hot stones into birchbark containers filled with sap. Sugar products were made by slowly stirring the syrup in basswood troughs. Candy was made by pressing the sugar into molds and letting it harden.

In contrast, today's commercial operations are highly sophisticated with miles of plastic tubing carrying the sap from the trees to the processing center. Vacuum systems speed the process and increase the yield.

The roots are in water instead of soil. Nutrients are added to the water.

Here are some suggestions:
- Select large trees, at least ten inches in diameter. Any of the varieties of maple will produce sap, but the sugar maple is the most productive; it is also sweeter than the others. Do not bother with diseased or rotting trees. If you intend to produce syrup to sell, it will pay to cut out other varieties of trees and any of the smaller maples which may crowd those you tap. About 80 to 100 trees per acre is considered ideal.
- Sap usually begins to flow in early March when snow is still on the ground but when the temperature rises to about 45°F by day but still falls below freezing at night. The run will usually last from four to six weeks.
- For convenience, tapholes should be about 4½ feet above the ground. Use a $\frac{7}{16}$th drill, being careful to make round (not oval) holes so that the sap will not leak around the *spile*, as the spigot is called. Tapholes should be about 3" deep for maximum yield. If the drill carries out red sawdust you have gone too deep; you have entered the non-productive heartwood. The drillings should be white.
- Larger trees may have more than one taphole; here is a rule of thumb:

Diameter of Tree	Number of Tapholes
10" - 14"	1
15" - 19"	2
20" - 24"	3
25" and larger	4

Avoid drilling into old tapholes.
- Hammer the spiles (they are available commercially) in snugly, but forcing them too hard may cause the bark to split and the tree to leak.
- The life of a taphole may be substantially prolonged by inserting a paraformaldehyde pellet into the hole when it is drilled. This will retard the formation of microorganisms which multiply rapidly until they reduce the flow of sap or stop it altogether.
- The sap may be collected in pails hung under the spile.
Covered containers are available which will help prevent contamination.
- When the sap develops a "buddy" taste, it is time to abandon the tree for that year.

The syrup may be processed out-of-doors as in days gone by over an open wood fire or on a cast-iron stove. Because the evaporation process is a long one, the savings incurred by making your own syrup will be greatly diminished unless the fuel comes from your own woodlot. Commercial processors prefer specially made "sheet pans" to iron kettles because the larger surface permits a more rapid rate of evaporation. The procedure may also be made more efficient by using three containers and ladling the sap from one to the next as it boils, with only the last kettle being used to make the final product.

Make the syrup of a consistence and flavor that best suits you. The ratio of sap to syrup will usually be somewhere between 28 to 1 and 40 to 1, depending on the sugar content of the sap.

Once you have made your first batch you will know why it is so expensive!

Marketing can be from your home, through advertising or in specialty shops.

MUSHROOMS

The popularity of mushrooms is increasing at a faster rate this decade than any other food. There are special marketing opportunities for some of the more exotic varieties such as:

shiitaka	porcini
enoki	puff balls
trumpet	oyster
wood ears	

On the other hand, there is still a good market for the more common cap variety. Species picked in the wild — such as morels — also bring a good price. Most species grow better in a dark, humid environment. Abandoned barns are a possibility.

Special care must be taken to avoid poisonous varieties.

The nearest university extension service is a good source of further information.

ORNAMENTAL PLANT CARE

When people go away on vacations they are often willing to pay someone to care for their plants — in their home or yours. Some may prefer to have you water them in their homes so that you can check on the house at the same time.

You may get leads from local flower shops, or nurseries, or a small ad in the local paper may bring results.

TREES

Christmas trees take from six to ten years to grow from seedlings to seven-foot market size — depending on the soil and climate. Irrigation and weed control will speed growth.

Seedlings can usually be obtained from state, or even commercial, nurseries at a fairly nominal price. Planting can be by hand (with a planting bar) or by machine (pulled by a tractor). The latter is essential for large acreages. Planting should be in early spring when there is normally plenty of moisture.

Three or four years after transplanting, trees will need to be shaped (pruned) by machete or power shears. This is done in June. Improper shaping can ruin a tree. Trim only the new growth.

In late summer, select the pine trees you will harvest in the fall and spray them with commercial green coloring. Spruce trees are not usually colored but sprays are available to hold the needles. Harvesting occurs in late October or early November.

The most popular varieties are scotch pine, Norway (red) pine, balsam and spruce.

A minimum of 40 acres is necessary to realize the economies of size of operation.

Marketing can be directly to the vendor (lot operator) or to wholesalers who in turn contact the vendors. For greater profit, operate your own lot. If your tree farm is accessible and convenient, many people enjoy choosing and cutting their own tree.

Wholesalers and vendors usually pay the grower half the cost when they pick them up (or are delivered) and the balance after Christmas.

Boughs from irregular trees may be sold to floral shops for making wreaths or for use as decorative greens. This is also an option for the grower.

Shrubs and trees for landscaping include such varieties as spruce, arborvitae, pines, ornamental shrubs, flowering trees, and shade trees.

Marketing can be directly to the consumer or to nurseries and landscapers.

Spruce and pine should be shaped, as with Christmas trees. In fact, if they do not sell or grow too large to conveniently transplant, they may be sold as Christmas trees.

Machines are available for transplanting even fairly large trees.

Seedlings are usually available from state or commercial nurseries at modest prices.

Weeding, fertilizing and irrigation will all speed growth.

Unless you are sure of your market, you may want to start small (5 acres).

Check with your county agent or university extension service for further information.

Trees used for lumber or pulp (for papermaking) take many years to grow to marketable size — most of a human lifetime — but they are an excellent legacy for children or as retirement income for those who plan far enough ahead.

An alternative to planting your own forest might be to speculate on timber property — even young trees 10-15 years old.

Trees used for lumber include all varieties of pine, spruce and cedar and several varieties of hardwoods including walnut, oak and birch.

Of the trees used in papermaking, the aspen (poplar) is the most common and it is relatively fast growing. There are experimental varieties that are usable in less than 20 years; most mature at between 30 and 40 years.

There are two significant risks when investing in trees: fire and disease.

"YOU PICK" FRUIT OPERATIONS

Many people enjoy picking their own berries and fruit. They have better control of the quality and because they are furnishing the labor and there are no middlemen — the price is right.

You can provide the opportunity on a few acres of ground. Strawberries, raspberries and blueberries are among the favorites. Depending on your climate, apples, pears, peaches and citrus fruits are also possibilities.

For further information about growing these items, contact your county agent or nearest university extension service. Nurseries may also be willing to share their knowledge if you buy the starter plants or trees from them.

The crop not picked by customers may be sold through a roadside stand or directly to stores or restaurants.

YARD CARE

Many people do not have the time, knowledge, or physical ability to develop the kind of yard they would like and are perfectly willing to pay someone who can do it for them.

"Yard care" can include everything from mowing the lawn to landscaping with rocks, flowers, shrubs and trees.

If you are short on knowledge, many community or technical colleges offer short courses or even career training.

Remember, your best advertisement is the appearance of your own yard!

A good riding mower can get you contracts with businesses, industries, churches, local governments, etc.

These same customers may be interested in having their sidewalks and driveways plowed free of snow in winter.

Part II
ARTS AND CRAFTS

A certain amount of talent is required for most of the following income extenders, but talent can be developed. With a little training and practice you may surprise yourself!

CALLIGRAPHY

This is the art of fancy printing or handwriting. The talent can be marketed to organizations, businesses, or educational institutions by creating certificates, diplomas, official documents, etc. A substantial business can be generated through modest advertising and even by word of mouth.

The skill is sometimes taught in community education programs or night classes at community colleges or technical institutes.

Selling plaques or frames for certificates may go well in conjunction with calligraphy.

CARVING

If you have some basic artistic talent, you could very likely learn to carve.

The investment in knives and wood is minimal. Wood carving classes are sometimes taught by hobby shops or through community education programs.

Wood carving is an enjoyable and rewarding hobby in itself but if the quality of your work is good, your products may be marketable. As with so many works of art, prices are relatively low for the time and energy invested but good work plus a reputation may command excellent prices.

Possible outlets for your work include gift and souvenir shops, floral shops, art stores and galleries and even flea markets.

Wood carving machines are available for making one to fifty replications at a time.

JEWELRY

The creation of jewelry is an interesting and challenging hobby and it can be financially rewarding. In addition to basic artistic talent, the skill of soldering is important.

Rings, bracelets, pins, belt buckles and earrings are examples of marketable art work. Silver is relatively expensive but there are cheaper alloys available. Semiprecious stones such as agate, garnet, turquoise and Tomsonite may be used.

Tumblers for polishing rocks and saws for cutting them are relatively inexpensive.

The most profitable market is for unique, one of a kind, jewelry. Reputation is as important as skill in determining market price. It is difficult to find stores that will handle amateur work but you may try inviting people to your home for a "jewelry party" or even selling at flea markets.

Jewelry making is sometimes taught in community education programs, hobby shops or in community college evening classes.

PAINTING

Painting through any medium (such as oil, water colors or acrylics) is a rewarding hobby but considerable talent is required for marketable works. Again, with so much art work being produced these days, reputation is as important as quality in determining price. However, most amateurs underprice their work.

There are many options for marketing: your own studio, at home, displays at restaurants or other appropriate businesses, gift and tourist shops, etc. Outdoor or community art shows are also options — also flea markets.

Artistic, quality framing (and matting where appropriate) will help sell the product.

Some amateur artists have found it more profitable to paint on unusual surfaces such as rocks, leather or weathered wood.

SEWING

Creative sewing of dresses or gowns for special occasions such as proms or weddings can be very profitable. Other types of sewing, such as making curtains and drapes, provide a minimal return for the time and effort expended.

Marketing is usually by word of mouth but small advertisements in the local newspaper may bring new customers.

Sewing machine sales companies may be as good a place as any to take lessons.

STAINED GLASS

This is a rapidly growing hobby which can bring a great deal of satisfaction to the artist. The products can be sold or used as gifts. Remember, when the products of your art or craft work are used as gifts instead of buying something for that person, that is also adding to your income.

In addition to artistic talent, the skills of soldering and cutting glass are important.

Marketing is usually through gift or tourist shops but you can always fall back on craft shows or flea markets.

There is also a demand for stained glass artists who can repair church windows.

WEAVING, KNITTING, NEEDLE POINT, ETC.

Artistically created items, such as a special pattern on a rug made on a hand loom, are marketable at a fair price, but "ordinary" items like rag rugs, needle point, etc., seldom bring an appropriate return for the energy and time invested.

Knitted items of clothing and afghans are more easily sold.

Of course, all types of handiwork do make excellent gifts, and that can save you money and thereby add to your available income.

WOOD PRODUCTS

Toys, cabinets, shelves, bird houses, yard ornaments, bird feeders and gun racks are examples of wood products that can be marketed. Another possibility is repairing broken furniture or other wood items.

Equipment can be quite expensive and may include such power tools as lathes, drill presses, power saws, routers, planers, etc. But if you enjoy working with wood, think of it as a hobby, and any products you sell are a bonus.

Some wood items are marketable through appropriate stores. A friend sells dozens of bird feeders to a store that sells large quantities of bird feed; another sells thousands of dollars a year of wood puzzles through gift shops.

It is not easy to find outlets for wood products, but once you have a reputation for good work, people will come to you.

Yard displays of your work will also attract business.

Part III
AUTO
RELATED

Americans have always been in love with their automobiles and that love can be translated into extra dollars for you.

AUTO RESTORATION

This differs from "Buy - Improve - Sell" in that it is more concerned with antique vehicles (those 25 years of age and older).

In addition to mechanical ability it will take patience to track down replacement parts, etc. There are, however, mail-order companies which specialize in parts for the more common older vehicles.

It seems the biggest market is for cars that were new when the prospective buyers first learned to drive. In other words, "baby-boomers" are interested in vehicles of the 1960's.

Well-restored vehicles are always in demand but the return on your investment — particularly for your time — will seldom be great.

BUY, IMPROVE, SELL

If you have mechanical ability and like to tinker with cars, good money can be made picking up used vehicles that may look run-down but are mechanically and structurally sound. A good polish or paint job, rust removal, steam-cleaned engine, necessary body work, thoroughly cleaned upholstery and a tune-up can turn a nice profit.

CAR JOCKEYS

These are people who pick up new or used cars in other cities for dealers in their community. Pay is usually by the mile plus meals in transit.

RV dealers will also pay to pick up or deliver motorhomes, campers, etc. Contact local dealers.

The pay is not great but the work is pleasurable.

CHAUFFEURING

Most smaller communities do not have taxi service or even good bus service to other towns. People without cars or driver's licenses are willing to pay to be taken shopping, to do business in a neighboring town, see the doctor, etc.

Don't be afraid to charge "enough" and let people know up front what it will cost.

Be sure your automobile liability insurance is adequate. Chauffeur licenses may be required.

Advertising in the local paper and by word of mouth should keep you busy.

COURIER SERVICE

It is likely that businesses and small industries in your town are in need of occasional deliveries or pick ups in other cities. It might even pay you to establish a regular schedule — like every other day — to the nearest metropolitan center or starting from a big city, run a "trapline" to smaller towns.

Delivery services in town for restaurants, pharmacies and other businesses is also an option.

DETAILING

"Detailing" refers to cleaning a vehicle to the "N'th" degree, inside and out — washing, waxing, cleaning underneath, cleaning the engine, shampooing the upholstery, removing stains, etc., etc.

Equipment you need might include the following:

>   water pressure cleaner,
>   shampooing unit,
>   vacuum cleaner,
>   steam cleaner, etc.

Supplies might include:

>   soaps,
>   shampoo,
>   wax,
>   sidewall cleaner,
>   stain remover,
>   scrub brushes, etc.

During the cold months of the year, a heated garage is essential.

Offer a variety of price options according to the amount of work the client may want done.

Advertise through the local paper and/or radio station. A yard sign is another good idea.

Contact new and used car dealers and offer to work on their trade-ins.

LIMOUSINE SERVICE

Limousine service is in demand for weddings, proms, anniversaries, celebrations and other special occasions. If your state has legalized gambling, you may be able to work out an arrangement with the nearest casino.

A new limousine is *very* expensive, but it is often possible to pick up a good used vehicle (possibly from a mortuary) for a reasonable price.

Liability insurance and a chauffeur's license are required.

RURAL NEWSPAPER DELIVERY

Believe it or not, this is a pretty good money-maker. Newspapers in your town or in nearby larger cities are anxious to provide same-day delivery service to rural areas, usually using your own vehicle.

Newspapers offset the cost by building up their circulation so they can charge more for advertising.

Sometimes this can be coupled with servicing newspaper vending machines or delivering "shopper" papers.

SCHOOL BUS DRIVER

All that is required is the skill to drive the vehicle and the appropriate license, but it also helps if you can handle the kids and enjoy being with young people. In some states there are age restrictions.

There is a fairly good turnover in bus drivers and waiting lists are usually quite short and names move up fast. Evening, weekend or extended trips are sometimes available.

School bus driving rarely pays a living wage, so it is important to have a compatible job.

STORAGE

In this day of apartment and condo living and multi-car families, there is a need in many families for garage or storage space.

An unused barn, garage or other empty building can bring in a substantial income — and not just for car storage. Boats, RV's, snowmobiles, etc. are all possibilities.

TUNE-UPS AND SERVICING

There are many people who do not have a great deal of confidence in large car dealerships or service stations, but they will come to trust an individual who is always there to care for their car.

Little investment is required if you specialize in tune-ups, oil changes, tire rotating, etc. If the customer knows you will check such details as belts, air pressure in tires, anti-freeze, etc., they will gladly pay a premium.

This could very well tie in with a car "detailing" service.

By controlling the number of customers you can be about as busy as you want to be.

PART IV
BUSINESSES
SMALL AND PART-TIME

As with all commercial ventures you should check with your insurance agent regarding the possible need for liability insurance and with governmental units about certifications or license requirements.

Don't overlook the possibility of tax breaks or the possible advantage of forming a little corporation. Check with your tax consultant.

ANTIQUES

The rules for making money in antiques are quite simple:
1. Search for antiques and buy them at a low price,
2. Restore or recondition if necessary, and
3. Sell them for more than you originally paid including the cost of restoration and reimbursement for your labor.

In searching for good buys, the last place to look is in antique stores. Good places to look include garage sales, flea markets, small towns, farms, estate sales, auctions, and foreign countries, including Canada and Mexico. Searching is half the fun!

In restoring an antique it is a mistake to make it "look like new"; the goal is to put it in good or usable condition.

Favorite collectibles include clocks, watches, glassware, snuff jars, firearms, jewelry, books, silver items, gold items, dolls, toys, furniture, duck decoys, fish decoys (for spearing), fishing tackle, etc. Old cars, boats and farm machinery represent another variety of antiques. It helps to specialize in one or a few kinds of antiques so that you can become an expert in that field. It is more profitable to be knowledgeable in a few areas than to dabble in all kinds of antiques.

It is easy to fall in love with antiques and end up just collecting them, but to make money, you have to be willing to part with them!

ANSWERING SERVICE

This is an ideal business for those who are home-bound or who live in a house where someone is at home nearly all the time. There are numerous entrepreneurs in most communities whose work takes them out of their homes or shops but they are not big enough to justify having someone to take calls at their places of business. Examples would include electricians, plumbers, handymen, small builders, insurance salespersons, estate planners, and others who work alone. Most of them recognize that it is better to have a warm, human voice answer the phone than taking messages on a mechanical answering machine.

One answering service can handle several clients. In these cases, the phone calls could be answered with something like "Community Answering Service; for whom do you have a message?"

APPRAISING

If you have a good sense of property values, you can market your knowledge by appraising homes, farms, lake cabins, land, etc. This can be a service for individuals or for financial institutions. In some states a license is required.

If you are knowledgeable about precious stones, jewelry, antiques, cars, etc., you can also market that service as an appraiser.

The pay is relatively good for the small amount of time it takes.

ASSEMBLING PRODUCTS AND OTHER WORK IN THE HOME

Small manufacturers sometimes keep their overhead down by farming out work to people to do in their own homes. The workers pick up the materials and then drop off the assembled product at the place of business. Examples of such entrepreneurs might include manufacturers of fishing tackle, electronic goods, plastic products, toys, etc.

Bookkeeping, typing, computer work, word processing, and sewing are other examples of work that may be done at home.

To solicit business you might run an ad in the local paper, target prospective clients with personalized letters, or — best of all — personally call on the entrepreneurs.

DESKTOP PUBLISHING

Modern computers and copy machines make possible quality production of newsletters, advertising flyers, pamphlets, stapled booklets, and even small books (such as cookbooks) which can be put together with plastic, spiral binding.

There is also a need for designing and providing copy for the above items.

Many organizations, churches, businesses, etc. have newsletters. They are often time-consuming and a real burden for them. In addition to publishing their newsletters, you may be able to contract for writing and designing them.

Another saleable service would be the bulk mailing of the items you have produced.

Equipment costs are moderate and coming down.

DIRECT SALES —
SELLING ESTABLISHED LINES OF PRODUCTS

For many years countless individuals across this country have added to their incomes by selling for such established companies as: Amway, Avon, Shaklee and Watkins.

The product lines vary all the way from soap to cosmetics to vitamins to foods. The above companies have built their reputations on quality products rather than low prices. All four companies provide excellent sales training and promotion for their workers.

There are many other less well-known companies that also organize small armies of salespeople. Some are reputable; others are not. If you are recruited to sell for one of these lesser-known companies, check them out very carefully. Are their products of consistently good quality? Does the company stand behind its products with refunds to dissatisfied customers? Is your commission large enough to make your efforts worthwhile?

Most direct sales companies are organized as "pyramids". If you recruit others to sell, you will be eligible for a portion of the sales they generate. As they in turn recruit additional salespeople, you will even be eligible for a portion of their profits. The danger lies in that too many levels of sales staff (all sharing the profit) may mean that the products need to be priced unreasonably high.

If there is a downside to direct sales, it is that the salesperson's zeal for his/her products and his/her determination to make money may result in a hard-sell approach which may unnecessarily turn off friends and relatives.

Some communities may require that direct sales representatives be registered or even licensed.

FARRIER SERVICE (HORSESHOES)

In most areas there are not enough horses to provide full-time work for fitting iron shoes; however, there is often enough demand for a part-time business.

In most states, at least one technical college offers the training.

Start-up costs are not great.

Advertise your skill through the local newspaper and by contacting riding clubs. (And you'd better like horses!)

Cows have hooves too, and a cattle hoof trimming business is sometimes operated in conjunction with farrier services for horses.

GARAGE SALES AND FLEA MARKETS

Garage sales are a good source of quick pocket cash. Few of us, however, have enough goods to sell to attract enough customers to get good prices. An alternative is to have neighborhood sales or ask friends to join you. Sometimes most of the homes along a street or in a neighborhood will have an annual sale about the same date each year.

Flea markets provide an opportunity to sell such items as arts, crafts, home-processed food, bake goods, wood products, woven items, etc. They are also great social occasions and can be a lot of fun.

Some folks make a profitable hobby of buying items at garage sales, auctions, estate sales, and flea markets and then selling them at a higher price.

FOOD RELATED

Many people do not have the knowledge or time to prepare food of special types or for special occasions. There is a demand for bakery goods, cakes, holiday foods, ethnic foods, preserves, sauces, pickles, wild foods, etc.

Marketing can be by word of mouth, advertising, flea markets, etc.

Cakes decorated for birthdays, weddings, and other special occasions can be a lucrative little business all by itself.

Catering of parties, conferences, board meetings, weddings, or the entertainment of guests in someone else's home is another example of making money with food. If you are not careful, it can lead to a full time business!

You can usually make a good profit and yet undersell restaurants because of low overhead (not needing a special building or expensive equipment) and using little out-of-the-family labor.

Caterers often specialize in certain kinds of food: fish, ethnic, barbecued, etc.

GUNSMITHING

Gunsmithing is usually a full-time occupation, with formal training offered at technical colleges; however, someone knowledgeable about guns can earn a good side-income by cleaning guns, doing minor repairs, restoring the wood pieces, bluing barrels, attaching recoil pads, fitting scopes, etc. If you sell parts or guns along with the repair work, special licensing may be required.

Business can be solicited by advertising, posting a sign in front of your house, word of mouth, contacting sports clubs, etc.

HOME LAUNDRY

In the author's experience, very few commercial laundries do a consistently good job. People who do not have the time to do their own will pay more than commercial prices for a job well done.

If this business works for you, it would pay to invest in a commercial quality washer, dryer and mangler.

Mending and sewing are logical extensions of a home laundry business.

Business may be solicited through community bulletin boards, newspaper advertisements and by word of mouth.

HOME BARBER/BEAUTY SHOP

There is something very special about having a personal barber or hair dresser. There are many people who will be willing to come to your home on your schedule for professional quality work.

This is a particularly good business opportunity for someone who is tied to his/her home for one reason or another and who has the training along with some experience. Because of the lower overhead you could even charge a little less than the going rate.

Capitalize on the home atmosphere by serving coffee and goodies and making the client feel comfortable.

Licensing may be required.

Another option, which may not be all that attractive to many of us but pays well, is to be on call for services to a funeral home.

HOUSE CLEANING

It may not be prestigious but it pays well. It certainly beats flipping hamburgers for minimum wage in a fast food restaurant!

The people you serve will usually provide the equipment and cleaning products.

It is truly a great service to those who don't have the time or the physical capacity to do their own cleaning.

An extension of this business is to work for insurance companies cleaning up homes or businesses that have suffered water or smoke damage.

You may advertise your availability in the local newspaper, mail a letter or simple brochure to prospective clients or personally call on them.

INCOME TAX SERVICE

Most people need help in preparing their income tax returns; unfortunately, most don't know they need help!

Although tax laws are numerous and sometimes complicated, tax forms have been simplified in recent years and instructions have been made more clear. A good creative mind and common sense are important assets for the tax preparer. Courses in tax preparation are sometimes offered by community education programs. H and R Block — the well-known tax consultant firm — currently offers free courses; they also employ seasonal help.

Tax consultant work is very seasonal, usually January through April. If you want more year-around work, consider such complementary services as check writing, bookkeeping, copy service, fax service, etc.

Newspaper ads may help bring you clients, but how you are perceived in the community is really important.

INTERIOR DECORATING

Consulting

If you have experience and have demonstrated good taste in decorating your own home, office or place of business you may be able to market your services as an interior decorating consultant. Home and business owners often look for help in choosing colors, textures, drapes, furniture, floor covering, ceiling treatment and art work. A consultant may also help find "best buys".

Decorating

There is also an opportunity to do the actual decorating: painting, staining, paper hanging, drapery hanging, etc. Skills and expertise are, of course, required.

Furniture stores, drapery departments, paint shops, floor and ceiling stores and other suppliers may be willing to recommend you to their customers. Advertising through the local newspaper or radio will help bring work.

JANITORIAL SERVICE

There are an increasing number of businesses, banks, churches, offices, buildings, etc. that contract for cleaning rather than hire their own employees. In this way they avoid the hassle of training, supervising and replacing personnel. Because they don't have to pay fringe benefits it may also be cheaper for them.

Although there is an increasing number of janitorial businesses, this is also one opportunity for part-time workers.

KNITTING

Knitting is a productive hobby. Most "knitters" create items of clothing for themselves, friends or family, but there is a market for knitted goods. Perhaps the most popular item is sweaters — particularly with an original design or pattern.

Marketing is usually by word-of-mouth, but a yard sign or occasional newspaper ad in the fall or early winter will bring results.

Knitting is often taught in community education classes or a local yarn shop could put you in touch with an instructor.

LEATHER WORK — SHOES/HARNESS

In most areas it has become difficult to earn a living as a shoe repair person or as a harness maker, but there is enough demand for a good, part-time business. If the work is done in the home or in a garage the overhead is low and used equipment (if you can find it) is reasonable.

A generation ago, shoes were rarely discarded until they had been resoled or repaired at least once. In today's affluent society they are thrown away when the first little hole appears in a sole. It would not take a lot of advertising, however, to convince even a small family of the wisdom of repairing shoes.

Shoe repair is becoming a lost art, but with reasonable ability, one could learn fairly quickly from someone who knows the trade.

Riding-horses continue to increase in popularity and custom or harness-repair work is in demand and can be coupled with shoe repair service.

MANUFACTURING — SMALL OPERATIONS

It is amazing how many large companies (3M for example) literally began in a garage or home basement. Our purpose here is not to help you start a major corporation, but profitable manufacturing can begin and stay small. Usually, some kind of machinery or equipment is needed and that cost can vary a great deal. It may be prudent to begin with good used equipment.

Here are a few examples of home-based manufacturing:

> fishing tackle (spoons or other lures)*
> plastic injection molding (toys, golf tees, fishing lures, utensils, souvenirs, etc.)
> punch press products (metal items such as fishing spoons, jewelry, parts for other company's products, etc.)
> Toys (wooden, plastic or stuffed)
> dolls and puppets
> novelty items and souvenirs
> machine shop work (perhaps contracting with a larger local company for their extra work)
> wood products (possibly using a multi-spindle wood carving machine to turn out duck or fish decoys, base ball bats, wooden art work, etc. As many as 50 items can be turned out simultaneously.)

If you are an inventor, you may wish to produce your own inventions.

MODELING AND TELEVISION COMMERCIALS

There is a demand in larger cities for models and for actors in TV commercials of all ages — and don't think you have to be particularly beautiful or handsome! Of course, for a speaking part in a commercial you usually (but not always) need a clear, crisp, pleasant voice. Commercials are usually produced by advertising agencies or public relations firms.

There are employment opportunities for part-time models in large clothing or department stores or by companies that design or manufacture clothing. Other possibilities include commercial photographers and advertising or public relations agencies.

If you manufacture sporting goods there is currently a 10% federal excise tax which must be paid by the manufacturer.

If you have the interest, use the yellow pages of the telephone directory, but apply in person. And don't give up the first half-dozen times you are rejected!

Once you have experience, develop a portfolio of photographs, film clips, etc.

OFFICE EQUIPMENT AND SERVICES

As stated earlier, if you have typing, computer and/or bookkeeping skills, there are probably small businesses or industries in your town who would be interested in hiring you to do such work at home.

Specific examples might include:

> preparing payroll checks,
> typing letters,
> tax work,
> keeping the company ledger,
> preparing bulk mailings, or
> recording data on a computer.

Modern computers and copy machines make possible quality desktop publishing of newsletters, advertising flyers, small books with plastic bindings, etc.

In small towns or rural areas copy and/or fax service could be provided in your home when it is not available nearby.

Although a newspaper or radio ad might bring you clients, it is probably more effective to call on prospective customers personally.

Basic office supplies could also be sold in your home as a supplement to the other services.

PHOTOGRAPHY

Modern cameras have helped many of us amateurs to produce professional quality pictures. With the help of community education programs or courses offered in technical or community colleges you can develop a marketable skill.

Opportunities to earn extra income include:

> wedding pictures,
> family and special events,
> graduation photos,
> passport pictures,
> pets,
> children, and
> Christmas card photographs.

There is also a limited market for photographs of a quality worth framing or for sale to the advertising and/or printing industry.

Cameras can be very expensive but there are now many on the market at reasonable prices that will do professional quality work.

Advertising will bring you business but it is the quality of your work that will determine whether you will stay in business. Don't go professional until you are sure you are ready. One possibility is to help out a professional photographer during those times of the year when it is hard to keep up with the business (early summer for weddings, pre-Christmas, etc.)

Suppliers and developers often put on special workshops for photographers.

PHOTO DEVELOPING

Owning and/or managing a 1-hour to 24-hour developing service can be a profitable small business. The technology is taught in some vocational colleges. The equipment requires a significant (but not large) investment. A convenient location is critical.

A good investment might be having several locations operated by graduates of a technical program.

PICTURE FRAMING

In communities where there are no picture frame stores there is an excellent opportunity for a home business, framing such items as:

> paintings,
> photographs,
> certificates,
> diplomas,
> awards, etc.

There are a number of suppliers of molding, mats, and other related items. They will provide directions and the minimal equipment needed. Some put on workshops. Community education programs may have helpful courses. It also helps, of course, to have artistic talent and good taste!

Another alternative is to connect with a professional artist or photographer and provide them with framing service.

Occasional ads and a tasteful sign in front of your house will tell folks you are in business.

PLAQUES-TROPHIES-AWARDS-ENGRAVING

Materials for producing plaques, trophies and other awards are available. All that is required to assemble them is some dexterity and creative talent. Awards produced by major manufacturers are generally very expensive. They are unaffordable for most amateur sports or tournaments. It is easy to compete.

Engraving (a tool is required) is necessary in this business but there is also a demand just for engraving.

If the quality is good and the price is right, there is a lot of business out there.

In addition to normal advertising procedures, contact bowling alleys, schools, recreation programs, rifle and trap ranges, etc.

POLLUTION AND HAZARDOUS WASTE TESTING

Pollution control today is big business. Independent experts are needed to test for pollution and, when it is found, to test to see if the clean-up is satisfactory.

The equipment required is neither sophisticated nor very expensive. Pollution control agencies and instrument manufacturers provide training.

Usually, states or local governments require certification. Contact your local or state pollution control agency for further information.

Testers are needed for:

>   asbestos,
>   air quality in homes,
>   oil/gasoline spills,
>   medical/hospital waste,
>   chemical contamination,
>   industrial hazardous waste,
>   water pollution,
>   testing drinking water, etc.

Your availability should be made known to schools, local industries, nearby units of government, etc.

Homeowners may hire you to test the quality of their water or check for noxious gases.

RENTALS

Advertising balloons, lights and signs

Businesses are often in the market for special advertising equipment for special events. Helium-inflated balloons, flood or spotlights and portable signs mounted on wheels are possibilities.

Sign making would be a good supplement to this rental business.

Bicycles and motor scooters

Rentals of these items are more likely to succeed as businesses in tourist or sightseeing areas.

Costumes

Costume rental is usually a year-around business, but could be limited to special times such as holidays like New Years or Halloween. Santa Claus suits are in demand before Christmas and bunny suits before Easter. Some items, like clown suits for parties or commercial promotions, may rent throughout the year. Drama productions by the community or schools are excellent sources of business.

This enterprise does not call for a large investment. Costumes can often be created or improvised from used garments picked up at garage sales or in used clothing stores.

Smaller items, like masks, hats or party favors, could be sold in conjunction with the rentals.

The business could very well be located in your home in a spare room, in the basement or in an unused garage.

Portable toilets

These are in demand for public or large private events — including reunions, sports events, open houses, etc. The business can be quite profitable and with modern units and equipment it is not as unpleasant as it may seem.

Water associated rentals

If you are near a popular lake, river or the ocean, there are numerous possibilities:

> boats
> canoes
> innertubes
> kayaks
> scuba/snorkel gear
> outboard motors
> electric trolling motors
> personal watercraft (like water bikes)
> wind surfers
> water skis
> body/surf boards
> fish houses (for fishing through the ice)

For some of the above, you could add further to your income by giving lessons for their use.

REPAIR SERVICE

It is becoming increasingly difficult to get broken equipment or other items repaired. Few stores who sell these items offer repair service; when something breaks, they want you to buy a new one!

Although a certain amount of knowledge and mechanical skill is required, there are basic courses offered at community and technical colleges and through community adult education programs. You will also pick up skills and knowledge as you go along.

A repair business could be located in your garage or basement.

Here are some possibilities:

> electrical appliances
> bicycles
> computers
> furniture (including reupholstering)
> lawnmowers

motorcycles and motor scooters
outboard motors
radios, television sets and VCR's
small engines (such as generators)
snowmobiles
vacuum cleaners

You may also do repair work away from your home. If you advertise your availability as a handyman who could do some of the following, you will very likely be kept plenty busy:

docks and boat lifts repairing: putting them in and pulling them out
lawn restoration and care
painting and staining
rotted board replacement
tile installation (floor, ceiling and bathroom)
roof repair
tree and stump removal
window repair, replacement and washing

RESTORATION

"Restoration" is different from "repair". It is more than fixing a broken part; it is returning an item to good, usable condition. It includes restoring antiques but also relatively new items. Here are some possibilities:

Automobiles

I have a friend who makes a substantial contribution to his income by purchasing used pickup trucks. He tunes up the engine, fiberglasses rust spots, replaces dented or badly rusted bumpers or other parts and gives the vehicle a fresh coat of paint in a current color. He has three or four in process all the time and seems to sell them as fast as he finishes them.

The same could be done with automobiles.

Boats

Old, wooden boats bring a handsome price when they have been restored. Even damaged or badly used aluminum or fiberglass boats can be substantially increased in value with a good cleaning, touch-up paint job or replacement of worn seats or other equipment.

Second hand boats sell best if packaged with an appropriate size used outboard motor and trailer.

Clocks and watches

Restoring older, antique clocks and watches can be a profitable hobby. Just finding them at garage sales or at auctions adds to the fun. The more modern electronic types usually aren't worth the effort.

Houses

Some people make a good living buying older homes in good neighborhoods and restoring them to attractive, livable condition. Older houses can be made "as good as new" by:

> replacing all bad lumber
> repairing or replacing windows in need
> giving the roof new shingles
> painting, staining or replacing the siding (consider metal)
> tuckpointing any brickwork
> refurbishing the interior (paint, stain, carpeting, etc.)
> landscaping the lot (very important!)

Sandblasting, Pressurized water treatment and steam cleaning

Sandblasting and pressurized water treatment are ways of cleaning the grime and pollution off brick or metal buildings. Steam cleaning is more appropriate for vehicle engines. Weathered wood or decking can be restored with pressurized water. These pieces of equipment can be hazardous to people and even to the items being cleaned, be sure you carefully read the directions that come with the equipment or, better yet, work for a time with someone who is skilled in their use.

A newspaper or local radio ad is perhaps the best way of informing local people that you are in business, but like any other venture, if you do a good job the news will spread by word of mouth.

SECURITY RELATED

In this time of increasing crime, security services are more and more in demand. The following are all possibilities — separately or in conjunction:

Locksmith

This includes installing or replacing locks of various kinds.

Alarm systems

These systems could be sold to homeowners and business owners as well as installed.

Vehicle security

Alarm or theft protection systems may be sold as well as installed in vehicles of all types.

House watching

When people are away on vacation or business they may be happy to have someone check their home regularly — particularly during the winter months in cold climates when there is also the danger of freeze-ups.

SIGN MAKING

Sign making can be as simple as hand lettering or as sophisticated as neon signs. A certain amount of artistic talent is helpful. The methods and techniques are sometimes taught in adult education programs or in technical or community colleges.

Hand lettering and numbering boats and snowmobiles is one opportunity.

Kits are available for making plastic signs.

Newspaper ads or circulars sent to prospective clients will help bring you work.

SPECIALTY SEWING

There is a substantial demand for "one of a kind" dresses for special occasions such as weddings, proms and other important occasions.

Although this business also will grow by word of mouth it may pay to run a few ads at appropriate times in the local paper, particularly when just starting the business.

Other kinds of sewing — such as draperies — are also possibilities.

SWIMMING POOL AND
HOT TUB CLEANING AND CARE

Most owners of pools — and even hot tubs — do not have the time or energy or know-how to keep the water clean and sanitary. They are willing to pay well to have someone else do the job.

Businesses which sell pools and hot tubs usually also sell the chemicals and other materials necessary for cleaning and care and will usually be glad to teach you all you need to know (unless they are also in the business). They may refer customers to you and vice versa. They will also be able to suggest appropriate rates or charges for your services.

A local newspaper or radio ad or a simple flyer targeted to pool and tub owners will also generate business.

TAXIDERMY

Taxidermy is a great sideline for the outdoors person. The techniques are not that hard to learn, but an artistic sense is mandatory. Correspondence courses are available and the skill is sometimes taught in community education programs. Another alternative is to apprentice oneself to an established artisan.

Some taxidermists prefer doing fish than game and vice versa and specialize accordingly.

There are some relatively new techniques like freeze-drying or molding fish replicas out of graphite which may be worth investigating.

Business can be generated by displaying your work at sporting goods stores or sports shows. A yard sign is also a good idea.

Practice on your own trophies until you are satisfied that your work is of a quality worthy of being shown publicly. Poor work will destroy your business opportunities.

TELEMARKETING

Most of us have been recipients of phone calls trying to sell us everything from magazine subscriptions to stocks and bonds. In most cases we are targeted; calls are seldom made at random. We are called by a stockbroker because our occupation, business or address indicates we may have money to invest. We may be asked to subscribe to an outdoor magazine because we have purchased outdoor products or belong to an outdoor type of organization. Prospect lists are developed and sold to marketing companies.

The targeting may be even more focused, as with companies that call regular or former customers for orders.

If you have a good "telephone voice and personality", a great deal of patience and don't mind being rebuffed by unhappy contacts — then this can be an excellent way to add to your income.

Check the classified ads for "help wanted" in this field. After some experience, you may be ready to start your own telemarketing business. Contact logical businesses and industries and offer your services. A married couple — friends of mine — began their telemarketing company just two years ago and already have seven employees.

Possible clients include:

> *banks* — advertising special services like seniors or loyalty programs
>
> *dentists* — reminding patients to have their check-ups
>
> *politicians* — taking polls, raising funds or getting out the vote (insist on a deposit to at least cover phone calls)
>
> *newspapers and magazines* — soliciting subscriptions or renewals
>
> *collection agencies* — making the first contact on unpaid bills
>
> *community fundraising* — reminding folks they have yet to contribute this year
>
> *schools* — checking on students with frequent absences
>
> *business* — special promotions, such as an invitation to an open house or soliciting orders from established customers.

In most cases, your client will supply the names and numbers to be called.

Most important, be careful whom you work for. Make sure they are legitimate and that the services or products they sell are of the quality represented. If you will be making long distance telephone calls, be sure you are paid regularly and frequently or have a pre-paid deposit.

TILE/CARPET INSTALLATION

Some of the best opportunities for carpet or tile installation are to be found through business places which sell these items but do not offer installation. Or - even if the service is offered - it may be fairly expensive because of general business overhead and it is not hard for an independent operator to under-bid them.

Few home or business owners have had experience installing floor covering or ceiling tile and will gladly pay to have you do it.

As you gain experience, you will be able to bid on larger, commercial installations such as industrial buildings, businesses, churches or government buildings.

Local newspaper or radio advertising is about as effective as anything you can do to generate business.

TOOL SHARPENING

Most of us don't have the equipment or know-how to sharpen knives, chainsaws, lawnmower blades, ice fishing augers, circular saws, or other tools. It is getting harder to find hardware stores that offer this service and when you do find the quality of work varies greatly. An earned reputation as a tool sharpener will bring you added income.

Little equipment is needed; the overhead is low.

Post your business card in stores that sell the items listed above but do not have a sharpening service. A yard sign, an occasional classified ad plus good workmanship will keep you busy.

TREE AND SHRUBBERY CARE AND REMOVAL

Here's your opportunity to be a urban lumberjack!

There is a demand in every community for:

        cutting down or trimming trees

        removing stumps and

        trimming or removing over-grown shrubbery.

Most people don't have the tools, expertise or courage to tackle these jobs themselves.

The equipment (chainsaw, axe, hedge shears and possibly a stump remover) are not expensive but you have to know what you are doing. Poor tools, power lines and toppling trees can be dangerous — but that is one of the reasons the pay is good! You will also need a pickup truck or good trailer to haul away the debris.

A newspaper or local radio ad will get you started; word of mouth will keep you going.

VENDING MACHINES

Most vending machines are owned by individuals rather than large companies. The profit comes from the sale of the merchandise contained in the machine. A part of the profit is shared with the business or owner of the building where it is displayed. The challenges are (1) to persuade businesses to display your machines and (2) to keep the machines operational. Courses in vending machine repairs are offered by some technical schools.

You can learn a great deal about this business by talking with store owners. Don't invest unless you have:

a good, marketable product

reliable machines

contracts to use the machines in specific locations

skills to maintain them.

WELDING

A welding service operated out of your garage, barn or backyard will probably keep you quite busy — especially in farming areas or any community where such service is not readily available.

For a retired welder, this can be a relatively easy and effective way to add to your income. Equipment costs are relatively inexpensive. Even if you are not a welder, for most people the skill is not difficult to learn. Training is usually available through community education programs or through a vocational or technical school. Although it is more critical that the weld hold, the appearance achieved by laying a good looking bead is also important. Some metals, such as aluminum, are more difficult to work with and considerable practice is required for proficiency.

A soldering service would be a logical extension of a welding enterprise.

A yard sign and an occasional ad will bring business; good work will be made known from mouth to mouth.

WINDOW WASHING

Most people literally hate washing windows. Even those working as house cleaners sometimes refuse to "do windows". This creates a tremendous opportunity for part time (or even full time) employment.

I have a friend who started washing residential windows in a retirement community to help pay his way through school. He discovered it was so lucrative he couldn't afford to quit! He tells me the secret is good soap (he uses "Soft Scrub") and a professional squeegee.

Difficult streaks are more effectively removed with crumpled newspaper than with cloth or paper towel.

A safe, sturdy ladder is important. An aluminum ladder is probably best. If heights are a problem for you, just agree to do one story buildings.

A local advertisement should bring plenty of business - especially during the spring and fall seasons.

WOOD PRODUCTS

Toys, cabinets, shelves, bird houses, yard ornaments, bird feeders and gun racks are examples of wood products that can be marketed. Another possibility is repairing broken furniture or other wood items.

Equipment can be quite expensive and may include such power tools as lathes, drill presses, power saws, routers, planers, etc. But if you enjoy working with wood, think of it as a hobby, and any products you sell are a bonus.

Some wood items are marketable through appropriate stores. A friend sells dozens of bird feeders to a store that sells large quantities of bird feed; another sells thousands of dollars a year of wood puzzles through gift shops.

It is not easy to find outlets for wood products, but once you have a reputation for good work, people will come to you.

Yard displays of your work will also attract business.

YARD AND BEACH CARE

Many people do not have the time, knowledge, or physical ability to develop the kind of yard they would like and are perfectly willing to pay someone who can do it for them.

Yard care can include everything from mowing the lawn to landscaping with rocks, flowers, shrubs and trees.

If you are short on knowledge, many community or technical colleges offer short courses or even career training.

Remember, your best advertisement is the appearance of your own yard!

A good riding mower can get you contracts with businesses, industries, churches, local governments, etc.

These same customers may be interested in having their sidewalks and driveways plowed free of snow in winter.

PART V
CHILD CARE

BABYSITTING

This is the old standby for part-time work, and babysitters are more in demand than ever. Teenagers and older women fit the stereotype of the "typical babysitter", but who is to say there are age or sex criteria? Parents' biggest concern is employing someone whom they can trust.

The sitting may be done in the child's home or in yours — it is often negotiable.

Although traditionally evening work, more and more there are opportunities during the daytime hours when both parents are at work or when one parent who is normally at home is away.

CHILDREN OF WORKING PARENTS (DAY CARE)

In these times when both the mother and father usually work outside the home, there is a substantial market for people who can do daytime sitting for pre-school children (either in your home or theirs). Also, because of safety concerns, parents are often worried about their school-age children coming home to an empty house. Many would be glad to pay for a place where their children could spend supervised time after school until one of the parents can pick them up after work.

If children from more than one family are involved, your state or community may require a license. Operating a Day Care Center for numbers of children is really more like a full time job. Some type of licensure is almost universally required. There would probably be regular inspections and rigorous criteria for the facility. It is, however, a way to add to your income — significantly.

Advertise through your local paper. If you are running a Day Care Center, appropriate signage and decorations will help attract business.

FOSTER CHILDREN

Many couples add to their income and at the same time perform an admirable and critical service by taking foster children into their homes. Foster parents are normally certified by the state or county and are paid directly by that unit of government.

Foster parenting has many of the joys and heartaches of raising your own children, but with an added risk of becoming mutually closely attached and then being separated by the social service agency. Also, the children often come from dysfunctional homes and may have associated problems. One had better be motivated by more than the mere desire to add to one's income!

For further information, contact your local or county social service agency.

HANDICAPPED CARE

Loved ones of the more severely handicapped persons — of all ages, including the elderly — often need help in caring for that individual, or at least an occasional break to get away from the associated responsibilities. Helping care for the handicapped can be a rewarding experience in more ways than financial.

In most cases, it would mean spending considerable time in someone else's home, but, sometimes, arrangements can be made to have the individual in your home. The latter may be desirable from the handicapped person's point of view; it gives them a "change of scenery".

Schools and institutions housing the handicapped also provide opportunities for part- or full-time employment. Certification is often required but usually is not difficult to come by.

Driving specially equipped vans or small buses to provide transportation for the handicapped is also a possibility. A chauffeur's license is required.

For employment leads, contact the schools or those institutions caring for the handicapped or your nearest social service agency. If your interest is in caring for the person in the home, try a classified ad. It may also be a good idea to contact social services.

NANNY

Nannies are usually thought of as women, but there are men employed in this role — particularly younger men. Nannies literally move into the home with the family to help take care of the children.

The compensation can be very good with generous benefits — including health insurance, free room and board, free travel, use of a car, vacations, etc.

Being a part-time nanny is a distinct possibility. The opportunities might include:

> Joining a family only during their vacations or travels to give the parents time for independent activities;
>
> moving in with a family for those periods of time when employment takes one or both parents out of the home; or
>
> helping out with the children when one of the parents is ill or recuperating, etc.

PART VI
CONSULTANT

Part-time consultant work is a natural for the retired person who has successful experience and expertise in almost any field. It can be a second income for others.

Make your knowledge and skills known to appropriate individuals and businesses in your area and be sure to let your former employers know you and your services are available. It may be helpful to develop stationery and/or a brochure describing your background and what you can do.

Be creative in thinking of possible employers. For example, a postal worker could provide information on efficient and economical shipping services to almost any business, industry, or institution that is a heavy user of this service. A law enforcement person could be a consultant to the private or public sector regarding safety and/or security systems. An educator could help a business or industry design its own training program.

There is an associated need for facilitators who have the ability to help a business or institution think through its problems or strategies.

Part VII
ENTERTAINMENT

There is a market for people who can provide entertainment for parties, celebrations and other special occasions. The occasion could be in a home or could be sponsored by an organization, business or industry in a commercial facility.

COMEDIAN/COMEDIENNE

Have you ever watched a stand-up comic perform on television and said to yourself, "I can do that?" Maybe you can! Practice on a few trusted friends or relatives and see what they think. You may be encouraged enough to volunteer your talent. Once you are confident that you are well received, you can begin to charge.

I have a friend who was quite successful just doing imitations of Phyllis Diller during the peak of that star's popularity. All comedians have to start somewhere; you can be quite sure their first performance was unpaid and was not televised!

DISC JOCKEY

If this is something you would like to try and you have a collection of popular music and a good public address system, make yourself available for free at parties, dances and other special events. If you find yourself in demand, it is time to start charging.

If you are a student, volunteer your services for school events and gain your experience on school-owned equipment.

MUSICAL ENTERTAINMENT

If you sing well or have experience on one or more musical instruments there are several possibilities for adding to your income:

> large churches often pay for soloists, pianists, organists and members of the church orchestra;
>
> join a dance band as a musician or as a vocalist, or organize a band of your own;
>
> perform as an individual at night clubs, supper clubs, or for special occasions, etc.

You probably won't make a great deal of money but there is a lot of satisfaction in knowing that someone will hire you or pay to listen to you perform, and this will give you an opportunity to develop and perfect your talent. Who knows where it may lead? Have you noticed how many vocal stars say they had their first experience in a church choir?

PERFORMING FOR PARTIES

Sponsors of large or special parties often pay for professional entertainment, including:

> singers
> instrumentalists
> magicians
> jugglers
> mimes
> singing messengers
> clowns, etc.

Again, you may have to start by volunteering your services, but, if you are good you will soon be in demand to the point where you can charge.

PART VIII
GOVERNMENT
RELATED

ASSESSOR

Part-time assessors are hired by townships and by smaller communities. Even counties and large cities need part-time help certain times of the year. The job description is, essentially, to estimate the value of personal and real estate property for tax purposes.

Most states provide study courses or seminars in preparation for an examination and certification.

There are, of course, full-time professional assessors.

Assessors are usually asked to provide their own transportation but are reimbursed for mileage.

Part-time assessors can also find employment as appraisers for financial institutions, real estate companies, etc.

APPRAISING

If you have a good sense of property values, you can market your knowledge by appraising homes, farms, lake cabins, land, etc. This can be a service for individuals or for financial institutions. In some states a license is required.

If you are knowledgeable about precious stones, jewelry, antiques, cars, etc., you can also market that service as an appraiser.

The pay is relatively good for the small amount of time it takes.

CENSUS TAKER

Every ten years the U.S. Government employs thousands of people to take the census. The job description is simply interviewing someone in each home or apartment in a given area and recording that information. Census takers are expected to provide their own transportation.

These are often political jobs and applications should be made to the local officers of the political party in power at the national level (presidency). You might also contact your legislator or congressman if that person is of the same political party as the incumbent president.

CITY AND COUNTY GOVERNMENTS

Part-time workers — particularly clerical workers — are hired from time to time by most local governments. It helps to have typing or computer skills. There may, however, be other kinds of work available such as janitorial, road maintenance and construction, painting, etc. Many cities, for example, hire students each summer to paint the curbs yellow where there is no parking.

Even townships have occasional need of part-time workers. The town clerk, for example, may be a paid position. Townships also hire for snow plowing, road maintenance, etc.

Apply directly at the office of the city manager or county administrator.

It may also help to contact the appropriate elected local official.

FIREMAN

In most small, or even in medium-size cities, firemen are called "volunteers", but in actuality, they are paid for their service calls and even for time spent undergoing required training and other time investments. Sometimes there are fringe benefits and modest retirement plans after extended service.

Firemen make a major contribution to the health of their communities and enjoy a special camaraderie.

Application is usually made directly to the fire protection unit and selection is often by the current members of the department. Training is provided by the department and by the state government. There may be age limitations and applicants are usually required to pass a physical examination.

Firemen are usually called into action by portable radio or other electronic device and are on call day or night (their regular job permitting).

FIRE WARDEN

Fire wardens usually reside in rural areas and are appointed by the town board or the county commissioners (depending on the state). Their major task is to issue burning permits.

Pay is minimal but a valuable community service is performed.

For further information, contact your town board member or county commissioner.

JURY DUTY

In theory, jury members are chosen at random to serve in county, city, district, state or federal court systems. In some states, however, appropriate court officers sometimes choose from lists of people who are known to be available to serve on juries. Technically, one cannot volunteer for jury duty, but it couldn't hurt to contact the clerk of court for the judicial system where you are interested in serving, if that is the practice

GOVERNMENT RELATED

in your state.

The pay isn't great but you will be performing an important community service.

OFFICE HOLDER, ELECTED

Although most elected local positions are considered to be volunteer work, nearly all of them provide a stipend — either by the meeting or for a given period of time (month, year, etc.). Examples of these positions are:

> town board member
> hospital board member
> city council member
> school board member
> county commissioner
> mayor

In larger cities, candidates usually run with party designation; in smaller or less-populated units of government, the positions are usually considered to be non-partisan.

In most states, legislators are considered to hold part-time positions and the pay is set accordingly. However, in some states one could live fairly comfortably on the income. They are identified with a party label.

For offices of a partisan nature, it would be helpful to first become active in the party of your choice or in behalf of a candidate before running for office. If you have not been politically active, begin by attending the precinct caucus (held every two years). At the caucus, seek to be elected as a delegate to the county, district and/or state convention.

For non-partisan offices, prepare by being a volunteer and leader in community activities. This will help you to become better known and thought of as a likely candidate for office.

POLITICAL PARTY ACTIVITY

The vast majority of political party activity is volunteer work. However, top party officers who put in a great deal of time are often compensated. Campaign workers who put in several hours a day may also be paid. Campaign managers are usually paid very well.

Paid jobs usually go to people who have put in many hours of time as a volunteer and have demonstrated their competency.

Most jobs become available during the 6-month period prior to elections.

If you have not been active politically, begin by attending your precinct caucus (held every two years) or by volunteering to work for the candidate of your choice.

POLL TAKING

Newspapers, radio and television stations, political parties, and candidates pay people to take polls — usually by telephone.

Businesses, manufacturers of certain products and others may employ poll takers to test public opinion. Even such national organizations as Gallup and Nielsen may employ part-time pollsters.

If you are interested in being a poll taker, contact the sponsors of published poll results or contact others that you suspect may be interested in sampling public opinion.

Pay is usually fairly good for the time invested and the work is quite interesting.

PUBLIC LIBRARIES

There is often a need for part-time workers in public libraries. Most duties are of a clerical nature and starting pay is usually minimum wage. It helps to have typing and computer skills but there are opportunities for other kinds of work.

There are periods of time which are busier than others — depending on the library — and it is during these busier periods that part-time help is needed.

SCHOOLS

Most schools, both public and private, have need for part-time workers, including:

> school bus drivers
> secretaries
> teacher aides
> school lunch workers, etc.

The pay and working conditions are fairly good, but it helps if you enjoy being around children.

Apply at the office of the person in charge of the school.

Part IX
HEALTH
RELATED

With all of today's concerns about health, health care and fitness, this field provides a number of fine opportunities to supplement your income. Some require training and certification, but most require only appropriate talent and experience.

AEROBICS - EXERCISE - FITNESS

To work in these areas you need to "practice what you preach". So — if you are physically fit and enjoy working out, this field may be for you. Opportunities include:

> teaching aerobics and other exercises
> teaching water aerobics
> supervising weight lifting and strength development programs
> teaching or supervising swimming. Lifeguard
> coaching and/or organizing walking-running programs
> coaching and/or organizing team sports

Place where you may find such employment include:

> the YMCA
> community centers
> swimming pools
> community education programs
> privately owned recreation or fitness centers
> resorts and conference centers
> self-employment (rent a facility and start your own program.)

Training required:

> It depends on the activity, but perhaps more important than training are knowledge, experience and skills.

Certification:

> Where required, it may be available through a YMCA or the American Red Cross. Requirements will vary from state to state and community to community.

To find employment, apply at those locations where the program in which you are interested is available; or start your own business.

HEALTH FOODS

Health foods and vitamins seem to go together. In larger communities there are health food stores; in smaller towns these items are often sold out of homes or door-to-door. Franchises are often available for national brands. There are plenty of legitimate products on the market but this is an area where you need to be careful of scams and frauds or unwieldy pyramid marketing schemes.

For ideas, check health food stores.

You might also consider growing and marketing organically fertilized foods (no chemicals) or chickens and other poultry raised "on the range" (not in confining pens).

HEALTH AIDE

Part-time work is usually available in hospitals, nursing homes and clinics. The better, higher paying jobs require training. This training can usually be found in community colleges or technical colleges and will take from a few months to a couple of years. The latter is really preparation for full-time employment. The health facilities themselves usually provide training for some kinds of employment.

If a job is not currently available, you might try volunteering a few hours a week until there is an opening.

MASSAGE SERVICE

It is difficult to find training in this field; the best place to learn is from a practitioner.

Massage service is offered in health clubs, resorts, hotels, or on cruise ships. It may also be an independent business available in an office or home. It may go well in conjunction with a tanning business. Some masseurs even make house calls.

It will pay to advertise locally. It will also be important to point out on these advertisements that the service is not sexually-oriented.

TANNING

There is currently a great deal of interest in paying for a "healthy tan look". The investment in tanning booths is relatively small but you may need to rent a business location instead of using your own home — although that is a possibility, especially in small towns or rural areas.

It will also pay to advertise. Encourage people to get a "head start" on their winter vacations, stress the importance of a healthy personal appearance, etc.

HEALTH RELATED

Part X
HOME AND PROPERTY INCOME

BED AND BREAKFAST

B and B's are a relatively new phenomenon that has spread across the country like a prairie fire. I have friends in Port Alsworth, Alaska, who even operate a fly-in Bed and Breakfast; it is accessible in no other way.

Although most Bed and Breakfasts are located in large homes, you can add substantially to your income with as few as two spare bedrooms. I have not heard of a single spare room, but why not?

Most operators specialize in a unique decor, such as antique furniture or "early American", and a tasty breakfast with at least one special treat — such as breakfast rolls, coffee cake or an unusual treatment of eggs or cakes.

A good location (easily found and near a point of interest) is helpful. Advertising can be through a state or national register of Bed and Breakfasts, a strategically placed sign or posters displayed in shops frequented by tourists.

Check for local zoning or licensing or health requirements and with your insurance carrier.

HOME RESTAURANT

Since this book is dedicated to part-time ways of supplementing your income, our suggestion here would be to operate a limited, specialized restaurant in your home — perhaps open only on Sundays or on weekends for breakfasts or for evening meals.

You may also want to feature a very limited menu such as fish or ethnic foods — such as a smorgasbord. Another alternative would be to be open only the month of December, serving holiday foods and beverages in an appropriately decorated setting.

Check for local zoning or licensing requirements and with your insurance agent. The local department of health may also have regulations effecting such a business.

Advertising locally through the newspaper or radio station will bring you business; word of mouth and good food will contribute even more to your success.

A home restaurant and a Bed and Breakfast could be a good combination.

RENTAL

A friend purchased an older home in good condition while he was still in high school. He remodeled it (doing most of the work himself) into upstairs and downstairs apartments. The rent paid for the home in a relatively short time. He then purchased a second home and let the rent from both houses pay for it. By the time he had finished his education, started a career and married, he had several rental units. I believe he ended up with seven in all —including an eight-plex. This was the most he believed he could handle as a side income without becoming unduly burdened with management responsibilities.

Rentals can be a good investment — providing you have "good" renters. The secret is to have quality buildings with relatively high rent.

There are several other rental possibilities:

> a spare bedroom in your home for a single person;
> remodeling your home to include a basement or upstairs apartment as a rental unit;
> investing in a government subsidized, low income, multidwelling unit;
> renting out your home or vacation cabin when they are not in use.

FARM RENTALS

As described in Part I, "Agriculture Related", a scenic part of the farm could be set aside as a campground or good hunting land could be rented to hunters.

Empty buildings are often usable for storage and may be rented to local businesses, industries or individuals. Be sure there is a written understanding as to who provides the insurance against fire or other damage.

Land that is not under cultivation may be rented to neighboring farmers.

STORAGE

There seems to be a shortage of storage facilities in most communities. An empty garage or unused portion of your home can bring you added income with little or no effort.

A good investment in many areas has been a mini-storage facility where a single story building is sub-divided into several private units. These are most easily rented in tourist areas or in communities with a large number of apartment buildings.

Have a written understanding about who provides the insurance.

HOME AND PROPERTY INCOME

Part XI
NATURE'S BOUNTY

Nature provides much that can be harvested for added income. Be careful, however, if you collect items from property not your own that you have permission.

CHRISTMAS WREATHS AND CANDELABRA

Spruce and pine boughs can be woven into holiday wreaths and marketed to shops selling Christmas items, to Christmas tree lot operators, or to organizations which can sell them as a money raiser.

Wreaths may also be made from cones and nuts, each glued to a round toothpick and stuck into a Styrofoam circle. They should be placed so close together that none of the foam is visible. A bow of red ribbon and a sprig of holly will add a special touch.

Attractive holiday candelabra can be fashioned from birch logs (about 6 inches in diameter), with holes drilled to hold the candles and sprigs of spruce or pine for added attraction. If the candles are allowed to burn down close to the wood they can become a fire hazard.

The candelabra can be best marketed through gift shops, Christmas stores and floral businesses.

CLAM SHELLS

Freshwater clam shells — particularly those from the Mississippi River and its tributaries — are in demand by Japanese pearl "growers". A particle of shell is implanted in each oyster. The pearl develops around the clam shell.

Although clams may be found in any depth of water, scuba divers have the best chance for discovering large beds of clams.

For further information, contact the Japanese consulate in your nearest large city.

DRIFTWOOD

Driftwood may be found on ocean beaches or along the shores of any large lake — especially wilderness lakes. It is used as decor in homes, as an accent in gardens, in floral shops for special arrangements and by taxidermists for game bird mountings.

Once you have collected a supply, contact the outlets suggested in the previous paragraph.

FIREWOOD

Many homes are heated by wood, and sooner or later the owners become tired of cutting and splitting their own supply. The best prices, however, can usually be "extracted" from urban owners of fireplaces.

Birch, oak and maple are favorites.

You may market the firewood directly to the consumer or sell to convenience stores and similar outlets that sell wood by the bundle.

You will probably need a commercial quality chain saw and wood splitter. A pickup truck or good trailer is also a requirement.

A local newspaper advertisement should bring you several phone calls.

FISH BAIT

Fishermen spend millions of dollars each year on worms, minnows and leeches. You can make bait available at your home or sell it to bait dealers.

If you don't have nightcrawlers in your yard you may plant them. They do require fairly rich soil covered by a healthy lawn. To harvest them, sprinkle your lawn heavily and then pick them after dark. Use a flashlight with red plastic or translucent paper over the lens. You will find the worm stretched out but with one end firmly planted in the ground. Seize the free end and hold it firmly. Do not try to pull it out of the ground until the crawler stops pulling. Keep them in moist bedding in a cool place.

Minnows may be seined or trapped in streams or lakes or raised in ponds. A license is required in most states and there may be certain regulations. Minnows keep best in cold, running or aerated water.

Leeches may be collected in most lakes, streams or ponds. The usual technique is to place bloody meat, such as heart or liver, in a perforated can submerged in rocky or muddy bottom areas. They are more apt to feed at night and return to their hiding places by daylight. Keep them in cold water.

FLOWERS AND OTHER BOUQUET INGREDIENTS FROM NATURE

Nature has much to offer to brighten the home or add to the decor, particularly during the fall, winter, or early spring seasons when cultivated flowers are not available from your yard. Here are some possibilities for off-season bouquets from nature:

> cattails
> dried flowers
> marsh grasses

NATURE'S BOUNTY

pussy willows
bittersweet
fungus
milkweed (pick green)
golden rod stems with moth bulbs
pheasant tail feathers

The items listed above may be sold to floral shops or gift shops — separately or packaged as bouquets. Flea markets are also a possible outlet.

There are some state and national regulations about picking wild flowers, etc., on public lands.

FURNITURE (RUSTIC)

Lawn furniture, such as chairs or benches, may be constructed of natural woods. If they are going to be used outside, the bark may eventually peel off; an alternative is to remove the bark and stain and/or varnish the wood. Cabin furniture is also a possibility, including such items as shelves, candelabra, birch waste baskets, lamps, chairs, benches, etc. These items may be sold from your own home or through appropriate gift or specialty shops or furniture stores.

GINSENG

Ginseng is a plant much in demand in the Orient (and more and more on this continent) as an herbal medicine or as an aphrodisiac. It grows in the wild and is usually harvested under state regulations, including seasons. There are ginseng buyers who will purchase the plant as is or it may be sold to health stores or oriental food stores.

LOGGING

In spite of the recycling of paper, there seems to be an increasing demand for wood pulp from which paper products are made. Although a variety of trees will work, aspen is the favorite. This is partly because it attains harvestable size so quickly.

There is also a demand for pine and cedar for poles, posts, landscaping timbers and for building log homes.

The problem for part-time loggers is that paper mills and major users of construction timber usually only want to deal with the larger suppliers. An alternative is to sell through larger loggers or deal with smaller mills and lumberyards. Another possibility is to invest in a small sawmill and produce your own wood products, including lumber, peeled logs and poles, etc.

Another related part-time business would be the pressure treating of wood products to prevent rotting.

MAPLE SYRUP

Native Americans were manufacturing maple syrup (and sugar) when European exploreres first came to North America.

Harvesting techniques were simple but effective. A deep slice was made in the bark of the tree with a knife or tomahawk and a cedar splinter was driven into the wound to serve as a spout. The sap dripped into a birchbark container at the foot of the tree. Before the coming of the trader with his iron kettles, the Indian boiled the sap in clay vessels or by dropping very hot stones into birchbark containers filled with sap. Sugar products were made by slowly stirring the syrup in basswood troughs. Candy was made by pressing the sugar into molds and letting it harden.

In contrast, today's commercial operations are highly sophisticated with miles of plastic tubing carrying the sap from the trees to the processing center. Vacuum systems speed the process and increase the yield.

Here are some suggestions:

- Select large trees, at least ten inches in diameter. Any of the varieties of maple will produce sap, but the sugar maple is the most productive; it is also sweeter than the others. Do not bother with diseased or rotting trees. If you intend to produce syrup to sell, it will pay to cut out other varieties of trees and any of the smaller maples which may crowd those you tap. About 80 to 100 trees per acre is considered ideal.

- Sap usually begins to flow in early March when snow is still on the ground but when the temperature rises to about 45°F by day but still falls below freezing at night. The run will usually last from four to six weeks.

- For convenience, tapholes should be about 4-1/2 feet above the ground. Use a 7/16th drill, being careful to make round (not oval) holes so that the sap will not leak around the *spile,* as the spigot is called. Tapholes should be about 3" deep for maximum yield. If the drill carries out red sawdust you have gone too deep; you have entered the non-productive heartwood. The drillings should be white.

- Larger trees may have more than one taphole; here is a rule of thumb:

Diameter of Tree	Number of Tapholes
10"- 14"	1
15" - 19"	2
20" - 24"	3
25" and larger	4

  Avoid drilling into old tapholes.

- Hammer the spiles (they are available commercially) in snugly, but forcing them too hard may cause the bark to split and the tree to leak.

- The life of a taphole may be substantially prolonged by inserting a paraformaldehyde pellet into the hole when it is drilled. This will retard the formation of microorganisms which multiply rapidly until they reduce the flow of sap or stop it altogether.

- The sap may be collected in pails hung under the spile.
  Covered containers are available which will help prevent contamination.
- When the sap develops a "buddy" taste, it is time to abandon the tree for that year.

The syrup may be processed out-of-doors as in days gone by over an open wood fire or on a cast-iron stove. Because the evaporation process is a long one, the savings incurred by making your own syrup will be greatly diminished unless the fuel comes from your own woodlot. Commercial processors prefer specially made "sheet pans" to iron kettles because the larger surface permits a more rapid rate of evaporation. The procedure may also be made more efficient by using three containers and ladling the sap from one to the next as it boils, with only the last kettle being used to make the final product.

Make the syrup of a consistence and flavor that best suits you. The ratio of sap to syrup will usually be somewhere between 28 to 1 and 40 to 1, depending on the sugar content of the sap.

Once you have made your first batch you will know why it is so expensive!

Marketing can be from your home, through advertising or in specialty shops.

MUSHROOMS

Be careful with this one; some varieties are poisonous. If you are not knowledgeable, apprentice yourself to someone who is. There is a market for wild mushrooms — particularly restaurants and food specialty stores. Mushrooms will even sell at flea markets. Morels bring the best price but the growing season (spring) is short.

PINE AND SPRUCE SEEDS

Both public and private nurseries are in the market for pine and spruce cones from which the seeds have not yet dropped. This means harvesting the cones just before they open and fall from the trees.

Be sure you have a market before you risk your neck climbing trees!

STONES, PRECIOUS AND SEMIPRECIOUS

Every state and province has natural, semiprecious stones which may be used as settings in jewelry. Although the stones may be marketed to jewelry makers, the greater profit is in the jewelry.

Among the more common stones are agate and garnet. Minnesota has a unique stone called Tomsonite.

Some areas have rubies and turquoise; others have gold. Very few amateurs make any significant amount of money looking for either precious or semiprecious stones or metals, but it is a lot of fun and can add to your income.

If making jewelry from your finds interests you, there are courses available through community or adult education programs. The investment (tumblers, polishers, small lathes, sodering tools, etc.) is not large. If you have difficulty selling your work, these items still make nice gifts, and that can save you money and thereby add at least a little to your income.

TURTLES

Snapping turtles are in demand as food by restaurants, locker plants, butcher shops, fish markets, etc. They may be harvested by trapping, set lines or by spearing them in spring or fall when they are in hibernation (usually in mud in relatively shallow water). Remember, they do bite!

Check state regulations.

For instructions on cleaning turtles, read *Nature's Bounty for Your Table* by this author.

WILD FRUITS, NUTS AND BERRIES

The seasons are short but the earnings can be fairly significant. Of course, it really helps if you enjoy picking and have learned to ignore mosquitoes, deerflies, gnats, etc.!

Market possibilities include restaurants, stores, candy manufacturers, bakeries, and — don't forget your less ambitious friends and neighbors. I have a good friend who barters blueberries for free restaurant meals.

People are also willing to pay a premium for wild fruit processed into pies, preserves, candies, sauces, etc.

WILD RICE

Although wild rice may be grown in man-made paddies for part-time income, small operations are rarely profitable.

In states and provinces where wild rice is grown naturally, there are seasons when it may be harvested and regulations as to how it may be done (size and width of boat, etc.).

The method of harvesting permitted in wild stands is usually that used by Native Americans for thousands of years: bend the plants over the canoe and beat the grain heads with a stick. The ripe kernels will fall into the bottom of the boat. Be sure not to harm or break the stems since the kernels mature at different times in the same head and the rice paddy can therefore be revisited in a few days. This is the reason narrow boats are required.

The "green" rice may be sold to processors or processed yourself. For more detailed information, read *Nature's Bounty for Your Table* by this author.

Part XII
PET RELATED

When we think about pets, we usually think of dogs or cats, but there are others: tropical fish, pot-bellied pigs, horses, birds, ferrets, etc. Each offers opportunities for part-time income.

BOARDING

It is often difficult, or even impossible, to bring pets along on vacations or extended travel. Pet owners will pay a good price to know their pet is well-fed and cared for. All that is usually required are kennels, cages or a fenced-in area. If the pets are likely to be noisy or smell, you would not want close neighbors; also, there may be zoning regulations.

There is also the option of visiting the pets where they normally live and feeding them regularly. This would require no investment on your part. You might couple this with watering plants while homeowners are away and just checking on the house to see if the heat is on, etc.

BREEDING

There is good money in stud fees and in raising and selling puppies, colts, kittens, etc. — particularly if they are registered. Just using your family pet in this business can provide some significant "pocket money".

It is important to use registered animals (you can charge much more) and to take care of that paper work.

Think about all different kinds of pets — not just dogs and cats.

EXERCISING

Most pets need exercising — particularly dogs and horses. Busy people will pay for this service. This is particularly true of pet owners in large cities.

To attract business, try the classified ads.

GROOMING

Pets including horses, dogs and cats require grooming. It is a chore most pet owners don't relish. The service may include bathing, hair trimming, nail trimming, delousing, farrier and hoof services for horses, etc.

Grooming can readily be combined with boarding, exercising and training businesses.

PET CEMETERIES

This could be a "biggie"! Pet cemeteries are becoming popular. The services go far beyond disposing of a dead pet. Caskets, headstones, monuments and even services may be included.

PHOTOGRAPHS AND PAINTINGS

Many people think more of their pets than some folks do of their children. They will gladly pay for a professional photograph or painting.

The key is advertising to plant the thought and to let pet owners know that you are available for that service.

Paintings are usually done from photographs (pets make impatient models), so you can solicit business by advertising over as large an area as you can afford.

PET SUPPLIES

This business will go well with any of the above or below possibilities or could stand alone. For dogs, you might include:

    dog food
    food treats
    collars
    flea and tick collars
    harnesses
    grooming instruments
    soaps
    beds and/or bedding
    wearable blankets for cold weather
    water and food containers
    toys
    dummies for teaching retrieving
    whistles
    shock collars (for training)
    non-prescription health items
For cats we would suggest:
    food
    food treats
    food and drink containers
    grooming instruments
    collars
    parasite collars
    bells
    toys

        beds
        scratch posts
        litter and litter containers
        non-prescription health items
For horses there are:
        bridles
        harnesses
        harness bells
        saddles
        food
        food and drink containers
        grooming instruments
        sleighs, carts and buggies
        blankets
        apparel for the riders

TRAINING

Obedience training is valuable for all animals.

Dog training may also include hunting waterfowl, upland birds and small game animals, retrieving, etc. Some kinds of dogs may be trained to pull sleds or carts.

Many horse owners need help in breaking or training their animals.

Few pet owners have the time or expertise required to train animals and will gladly pay for professional help.

Training usually means educating the owners as well as working with the pets.

Training would fit well with several of the pet businesses already mentioned.

Part XIII
RECREATION AND SPORTS RELATED

AIR TAXI SERVICE AND RIDES

If you happen to own a plane, you may sell rides during community celebrations or on appropriate holidays. Another possibility is to develop an air taxi service delivering passengers and small freight items to communities without commercial air service.

When charging for rides, be sure you are covered by insurance.

BOAT RELATED

Options include:
> boat rentals
> boat rides
> boat restoration
> boat and motor repair
> boat detailing
> painting on boat license numbers

ENTERING SPORTS CONTESTS

Monetary prizes are sometimes offered for contests in such sports as:
> golf
> fishing
> running
> trap and skeet shooting
> automobile races
> snowmobile races
> boat races

FISHING, HUNTING AND CAMPING ON PRIVATE LAND

There are several possibilities:

1. Many city folks would like the experience of living on a farm - especially for their children or grandchildren. A week or two on an operating farm can be a rewarding vacation. These people want to experience living in a farmhouse, eating their meals with a farm family, and trying hands-on agriculture. Farms with livestock are the most popular. The

charge may be comparable to what it would cost to stay at a resort.

2. If your farm includes a fishing lake, many people will pay for the opportunity to fish it. You may charge by the hour or by the pound or some combination thereof.

3. If you can provide duck, goose, pheasant or deer hunting, there are many hunters who will gladly pay for privacy and exclusive hunting privileges.

4. Campground development may also bring you added income. Some campers prefer these smaller, more private campsites. However, some may expect electricity, water, and even sewer hookups. These can be expensive. Also, check with local authorities (county or township) for possible licensing requirements and other regulations.

FISH PONDS — FOR FOOD AND FOR SPORT

Natural ponds or even those created by heavy equipment can produce a profitable crop of fish. Good fishing in lakes and streams is hard to come by these days. People are willing to pay a good price to fish ponds well-stocked with trout, bass, panfish, catfish and even bullheads. Parents are particularly anxious to provide this opportunity for their children — or grandchildren. The charge is usually by the hour with an additional charge for those fish kept.

There is also a good commercial market for fish — particularly trout, perch and catfish. These can be netted or seined from the ponds.

Large ponds or small lakes may generate their own food for the fish, but commercial food is available. Fish add more weight per pound of food consumed than any variety of livestock. Some kinds of fish, like northern pike or walleye, prefer live food — such as minnows. They are, however, slow-growing compared to other varieties and relatively difficult to raise.

In cold climates, shallow ponds will freeze-out in winter unless aerated. Commercial aerators are available but are fairly expensive; however, old vacuum cleaners with a reversed action will do just fine.

University extension services are usually good sources for further information about growing fish. You should also check with your local Department of Natural Resources regarding possible licensing and other regulations.

GUIDE SERVICE

Guides are hired for all sorts of activities, including:
>   fishing
>   hunting
>   exploring
>   spelunking (exploring caves)
>   rafting
>   canoeing

trail riding
sightseeing (including foreign as well as domestic
    tourists)

Advertise your availability where related equipment is sold or in businesses frequented by tourists. Let local travel agencies know about your service.

LAKE ACCESS, PLOWING SNOW IN WINTER

When there is heavy snow, fishermen expect to pay for plowed access to a lake. This is a particularly appropriate venture if you already have a truck and plow for your own needs or for plowing out others' driveways or parking areas.

LIFEGUARD

Pools and swimming beaches hire part-time lifeguards. Red Cross lifesaving certification is usually required.

MANUFACTURING

It is amazing how many large companies (3M for example) literally began in a garage or home basement. Our purpose here is not to help you start a major corporation, but profitable manufacturing can begin and stay small. Usually, some kind of machinery or equipment is needed and that cost can vary a great deal. It may be prudent to begin with good, used equipment.

Here are a few examples of home-based manufacturing:
fishing tackle (spoons or other lures)*
plastic injection molding (toys, golf tees, fishing lures,
    utensils, souvenirs, etc.)
punch press products (metal items such as fishing
    spoons, jewelry, parts for other company's products,
    etc.)
Toys (wooden, plastic or stuffed)
dolls and puppets
novelty items and souvenirs
machine shop work (perhaps contracting with a larger
    local company for their extra work)
wood products (possibly using a multi-spindle wood
    carving machine to turn out duck or fish decoys,
    baseball bats, wooden art work, etc. As many as 50
    items can be turned out simultaneously.)
If you are an inventor, you may wish to produce your own inventions.

If you manufacture sporting goods there is currently a 10% federal excise tax which must be paid by the manufacturer.

REPAIR SERVICE

It is becoming increasingly difficult to get broken equipment or other items repaired. Few stores who sell these items offer repair service; when something breaks, they want you to buy a new one!

Although a certain amount of knowledge and mechanical skill is required, there are basic courses offered at community and technical colleges and through community adult education programs. You will also pick up skills and knowledge as you go along.

A repair business could be located in your garage or basement.

Here are some possibilities:

> electrical appliances
> bicycles
> computers
> furniture (including reupholstering)
> lawnmowers
> motorcycles and motor scooters
> outboard motors
> radios, television sets and VCR's
> small engines (such as generators)
> snowmobiles
> vacuum cleaners

You may also do repair work away from your home. If you advertise your availability as a handyman who could do some of the following, you will very likely be kept plenty busy:

> docks and boat lifts repairing: putting them in and pulling them out
> lawn restoration and care
> painting and staining
> rotted board replacement
> tile installation (floor, ceiling and bathroom)
> roof repair
> tree and stump removal
> window repair, replacement and washing

SPORTS

There are a number of extra income-generating activities associated with competitive sports, including:

> coaching
> refereeing
> working at sports events (timing, taking tickets, etc.)
> youth camps that are sports-related
> private lessons (golf, weight lifting, tennis, etc.)
> sports reporting for a newspaper

Experience in, or at least a good knowledge of, the sport is assumed. Prospective employers include schools, professional sports events, youth camps, recreation programs, etc. Private lessons would probably be paid for by the individual. Your local newspaper, if it is not large enough to hire a sports writer, may be interested in having you cover the local scene.

SPORTS EQUIPMENT, MANUFACTURING, RENTAL AND REPAIR

Bicycle and Motor Scooter Rentals

Rentals of these items are more likely to succeed as businesses in tourist or sightseeing areas.

Water Associated Rentals

If you are near a popular lake, river or the ocean, there are numerous possibilities:

boats
canoes
innertubes
kayaks
scuba/snorkel gear
outboard motors
electric trolling motors
personal watercraft (like water bikes)
wind surfers
water skis
body/surf boards
fish houses (for fishing through the ice)

For some of the above, you could add further to your income by giving lessons for their use.

PART XIV
TEACHING
(Non-Professional)

There are many opportunities in teaching that are not classroom related which may provide opportunities for you to add to your income. Certification is rarely a problem. Here are some examples:

      arts and crafts, ceramics, etc.
      baton twirling
      CPR
      cake decorating
      dancing (ballet, square, ballroom, line, etc.)
      figure skating
      hobbies (such as painting, photography, jewelry, etc.)
      music, both instrumental and vocal
      scuba diving

Prospective employers include:

      adult education programs in technical or community colleges
      community education programs (local school district)
      yourself — in your own business

PART XV
WORKING PART-TIME
OUTSIDE THE HOME

WORKING PART-TIME OUTSIDE THE HOME

There are many opportunities for part-time employment in every community, including:

church choir director
church soloists
church organist or pianist
church secretary
organization secretary
township clerk
retail sales
restaurant work
janitor work
substituting for people who are ill or on vacation
organizer for an action group or organization
desk clerk in a motel or hotel
helping with health club activities
temporary office worker

PART XVI
WRITING

WRITING

Being an author for a book such as this may be a longshot in your mind but it happens every day. You may sell your work to a publisher or be your own publisher — that is, investing in the printing of your own book and distributing it yourself.

If you like to write, part-time income can also be generated by:

        articles for magazines
        columns for newspapers
        newsletters
        reporting on local or special events
        script writing for a local radio or TV station

PART XVII
MISCELLANEOUS

ENTERING CONTESTS

Entering the contests you see or hear advertised can add to your income. After all — somebody has to win — right? Lottery contests, such as Publishers Clearing House really are a longshot, but essay or slogan contests give you much better odds. Far fewer people enter and skill is involved. I know a person who has won cars, foreign and domestic travel, appliances, cash, etc. Her advice is to be creative, accurate, original and sincere. Try to understand what the contest sponsors are looking for. She also warns, "Never enter a contest that asks you for money!"

PART XVIII
FINAL
CONSIDERATIONS

MARKETING

Whether it is:

marketing your product,
marketing your skills, or
marketing your services;

marketing makes all the difference in terms of your success or failure.

You may have the best product, but if no one hears about it, it will never sell. You may be a highly skilled technician, but if you don't tell somebody, you'll never be hired. You may be the most knowledgeable income tax expert in town, but if others do not know this, you won't ever have a client. So — how do you market your product or yourself?

ADVERTISING

In rural areas, the weekly newspaper may be your best vehicle, but a local radio station may also be appropriate. Use short, eye-catching or ear-catching, creative pieces. A lawn sign may be appropriate, but don't do it yourself! Hire a professional. A sloppy sign will scare people away.

BROCHURES

They are cheap — but don't do them yourself. Hire a professional. Focus the distribution on potential customers; do not use random distribution.

DIRECT MAIL

Cost effective only if focused on potential customers.

DISTRIBUTORS

A very effective way of getting your product into stores or catalogs, but they will expect a share of the profit for their services.

LIABILITY

Check with your insurance company if there is any danger of your being sued because of a faulty product, poor service or whatever. It is a small price to pay for peace of mind.

INCORPORATING

It costs only a few hundred dollars to form a corporation if you are starting a business. Why incorporate? There may be liability and tax advantages. Check with your attorney and/or CPA.

TAX CONSIDERATIONS

Keep good records. Generally, there are tax credits for the costs of doing business. Keep a record of travel, costs of materials and supplies, hired labor, entertainment, telephone charges, shipping costs, etc., etc.

Check with your tax consultant before you start.

HIRED LABOR

The law is quite specific about the employer's responsibilities for tax, social security and possibly other deductions. Because these regulations change from time to time we will not list them here. Check with your tax consultant.

EXCISE TAXES

If you manufacture certain luxury items, sporting goods, etc. you are required to file a form 720 quarterly and pay an excise tax. You must include this in fixing the cost of your product.

SALES TAX

Sales taxes vary from state to state and in some cases by community. You are required to collect a fixed percentage for the government on the cost of goods sold directly to the consumer.

PATENTS AND COPYRIGHTS

If you have an invention or unique product, it would be wise to apply for a patent. Check with an attorney for the names of consultants in this area.

It is against the law to copy somebody else's work.

Writing and music can be copyrighted with the Library of Congress, Washington, D.C. The charge is small.

Again, it is against the law to use someone else's work without their permission.

FINAL CONSIDERATIONS

CHOOSING A NAME

If you are starting a business, you will need a name. This is very important. Give it careful thought. Choose a name that will create a positive image; that will identify or help sell the product or service.

If you are the only person in the business, you may want to use your name in some way.

TEST THE MARKET

Don't invest a lot of money until you know your product or service will sell. Start small. "Test the waters".

Consult with your banker. They are specialists in predicting whether your idea will make money. Don't go heavily in debt.

HOW MUCH TO CHARGE

Setting a price on your goods or services is not easy, but most beginners set the price too low. Cheap prices indicate cheap products or poor services.

Include enough so that you are reimbursed for your labor.

If your venture doesn't pay you at least minimum wage, you may be better off going to work for someone else.

ENJOY WHAT YOU ARE DOING

In most cases this added income is really a second job. A full time job takes a great deal of energy. If you add other responsibilities you had better enjoy them or you will soon burn out. On the other hand, if the added work is fun, it will make your life that much more enjoyable and rewarding.

LOCATION

For most businesses, location is important. If you are working out of your home, you must make it easy for people to find.

If you rent space, you will probably get what you pay for.

Exposure to traffic (foot or auto) is important.

KEEP GOOD RECORDS

This is important not only for tax purposes, but also if you are going to know how much you have to charge if you are going to have a fair return on your investment, time, skill, labor and creativity.

BUSINESS HOURS

People must know when you are available and be able to contact you. If you are gone a lot, you may need a telephone answering machine.

If you post hours, keep them.

MATERIALS, SUPPLIES, TOOLS AND EQUIPMENT

Use good quality in all of the above. Poor tools and equipment will cost you dearly in the end.

If you use poor materials in your products, customers will be disappointed.

DON'T GIVE UP!

Success may not come until your second or tenth try.

Learn from your mistakes.

NOTES

NOTES

NOTES